Commun...

Tongue
Twisters

Dona Herweck Rice

Publishing Credits

Rachelle Cracchiolo, M.S.Ed., *Publisher*
Conni Medina, M.A.Ed., *Managing Editor*
Nika Fabienke, Ed.D., *Series Developer*
June Kikuchi, *Content Director*
Michelle Jovin, M.A., *Assistant Editor*
Lee Aucoin, *Senior Graphic Designer*

TIME For Kids and the TIME For Kids logo are registered trademarks of TIME Inc. Used under license.

Image Credits: All images from iStock and/or Shutterstock.

All companies and products mentioned in this book are registered trademarks of their respective owners or developers and are used in this book strictly for editorial purposes; no commercial claim to their use is made by the author or the publisher.

Library of Congress Cataloging-in-Publication Data

Names: Rice, Dona, author.
Title: Communicate! : tongue twisters / Dona Herweck Rice.
Description: Huntington Beach, CA : Teacher Created Materials, 2017. | Series: Time for kids
Identifiers: LCCN 2017017018 (print) | LCCN 2017031127 (ebook) | ISBN 9781425853396 (eBook) | ISBN 9781425849658 (pbk.)
Subjects: LCSH: Tongue twisters--Juvenile literature.
Classification: LCC PN6371.5 (ebook) | LCC PN6371.5 .R48 2017 (print) | DDC 818/.602--dc23
LC record available at https://lccn.loc.gov/2017017018

Teacher Created Materials
5301 Oceanus Drive
Huntington Beach, CA 92649-1030
http://www.tcmpub.com
ISBN 978-1-4258-4965-8
© 2018 Teacher Created Materials, Inc.

Table of Contents

Twisted!

Five friends faced forward on the first Friday in February. They were there for the Tongue Twister Take Down.

Trey trilled, "Time to twist!"

Shawn shouted, "She sells seashells by the seashore!"

Pippa piped, "Peter Piper picked a peck of pickled peppers."

Regis replied, "Red leather, yellow leather."

Quinn **quipped**, "Quick kiss, quick kiss, quick kiss!"

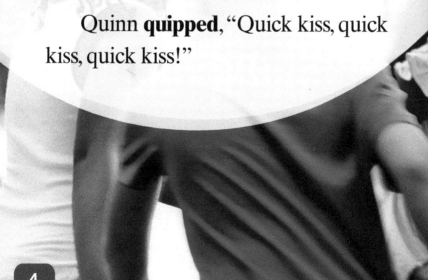

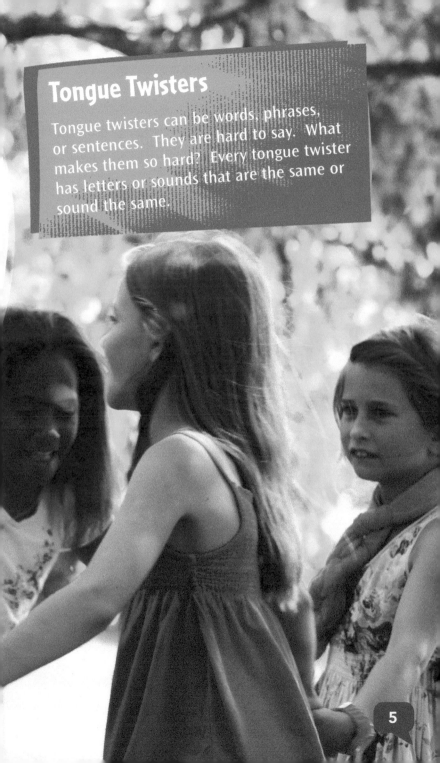

Tongue Twisters

Tongue twisters can be words, phrases, or sentences. They are hard to say. What makes them so hard? Every tongue twister has letters or sounds that are the same or sound the same.

The friends twisted on and on. They mumbled and **stumbled**. Finally, their tongues were too tied to say another word. Then, they just laughed.

Many people think tongue twisters are fun to say. They like the challenge! People want to see if they can say a tongue twister without getting **tongue-tied**. But the faster they speak, the harder it is.

Three Times, Fast

It is not enough to say a tongue twister once. To make it harder, try to say the tongue twister three times, fast! If you can say it quickly (and correctly) three times in a row, you have mastered that tongue twister!

Tongue Twister

"The blue bluebird blinks."

Can a Tongue Twist?

What happens when people say tongue twisters? Do their tongues really twist? No, there is no twisting. The sounds of the words are usually similar. That makes it hard for speakers to say them correctly. It sounds as though the speaker's tongue gets twisted!

Tongue Twister

"How much wood would a woodchuck chuck if a woodchuck could chuck wood?"

"How much wood could a chuckwood..."

Even a person who usually has no trouble speaking may have a hard time with a tongue twister. The words may not come out clearly. The person may have to speak very slowly to get the words out. The brain seems to tell the person the right thing to say. But the mouth does not say the right words! The words come out **jumbled** and mixed up.

Brain Power

There are billions of nerve cells in every person's brain. Those nerves send signals to the rest of the body. They control all the things we say and do.

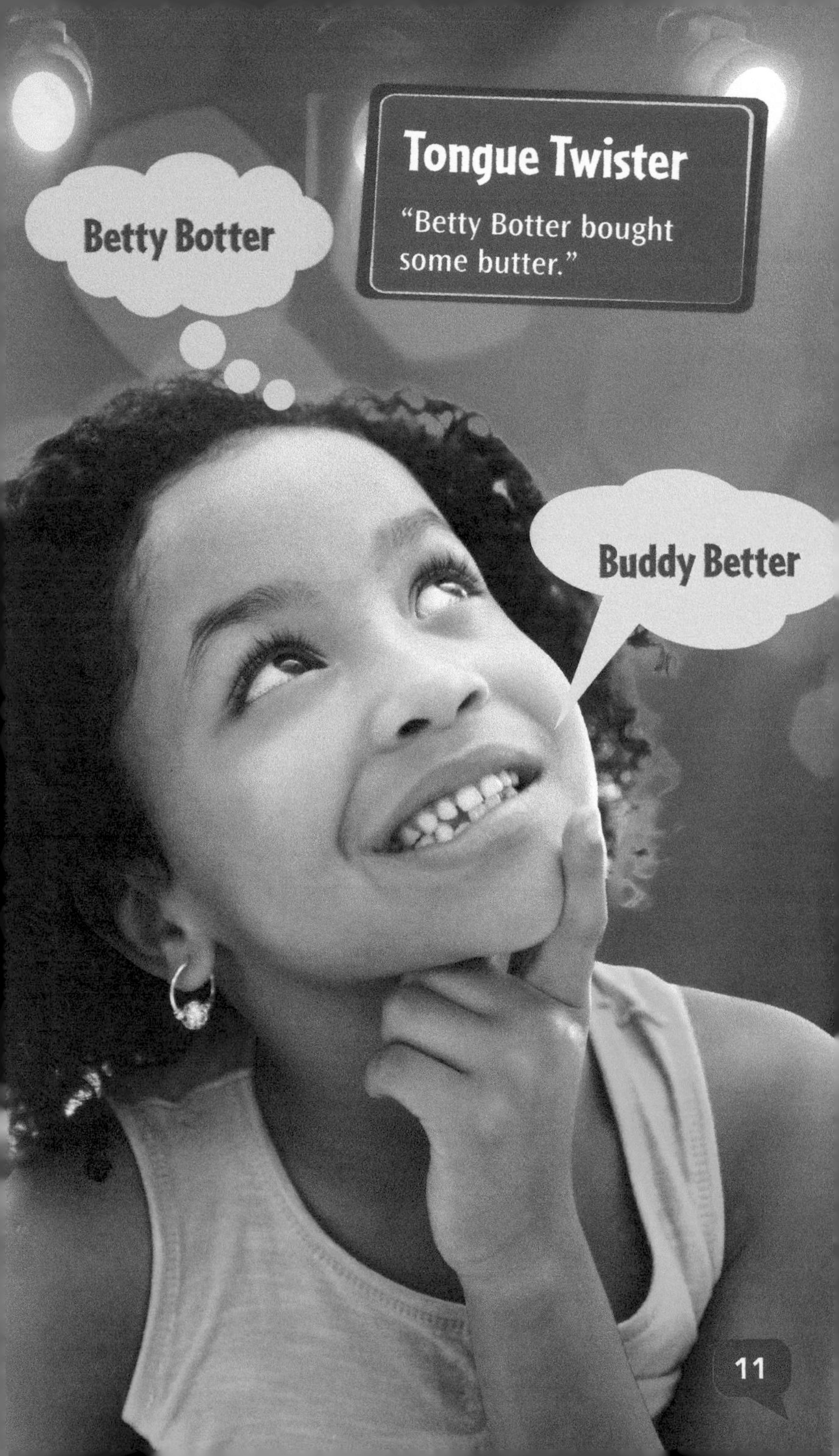

Tongue Twister

"Betty Botter bought some butter."

The Science of Twisting

To understand tongue twisters, you first need to know how humans make sound. It takes the brain, mouth, lungs, and larynx (LAYR-inks), or voice box, to speak. The larynx is an **organ** in the throat. It forms a type of passage to the lungs. Air flows through the passage as people breathe and speak.

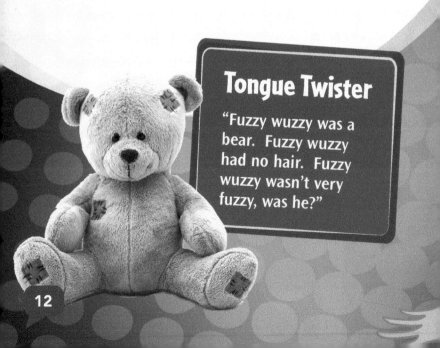

Tongue Twister

"Fuzzy wuzzy was a bear. Fuzzy wuzzy had no hair. Fuzzy wuzzy wasn't very fuzzy, was he?"

Down the "Wrong Pipe"

The larynx rises when a person gets ready to swallow. This keeps food and liquids from going down into the lungs. What if food tries to make it past the larynx? A natural **instinct** helps to keep people from choking. They cough!

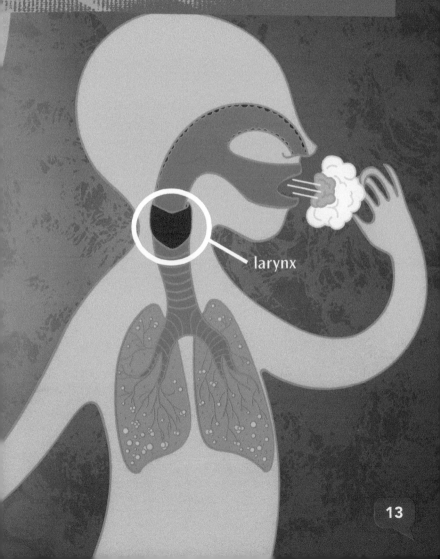

larynx

Inside the larynx are vocal cords. When a person speaks, these vocal cords move closer together. Air comes out of the lungs and makes the vocal cords move quickly back and forth. This helps to create sound.

Look inside a piano when it is played. The wires inside it **vibrate**. You can also see guitar strings vibrate when they are strummed. The vibration makes sound. This is true for vocal cords as well.

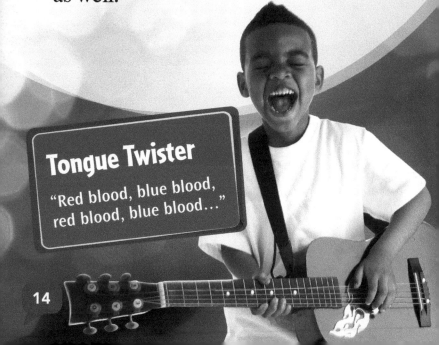

Tongue Twister

"Red blood, blue blood, red blood, blue blood..."

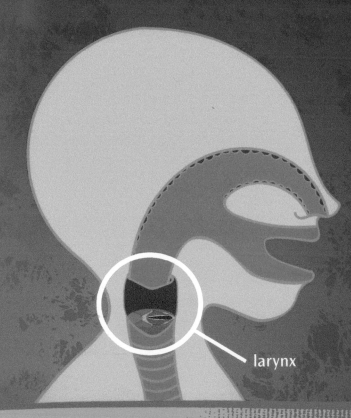

larynx

Vocal Cords

open

closed

The Brain Says, "Speak!"

When a person wants to speak, the brain sends signals to the larynx. It tells the larynx what to do. It also controls the pitch, or how high or low the sound is. Each person has a normal vocal pitch. It is different for every person. That is why some people have a high voice and some people have a low voice.

Tongue Twister

"A proper copper coffee pot"

Next, signals are sent from the brain to the mouth. That is because the sounds a person makes are formed in the mouth. The teeth, tongue, lips, and palate all play important parts. The palate is the roof of the mouth. All these parts work together to make the sounds people say to form speech.

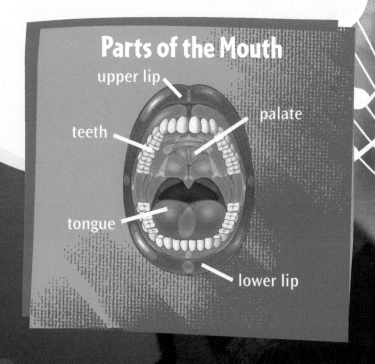

Parts of the Mouth

upper lip

palate

teeth

tongue

lower lip

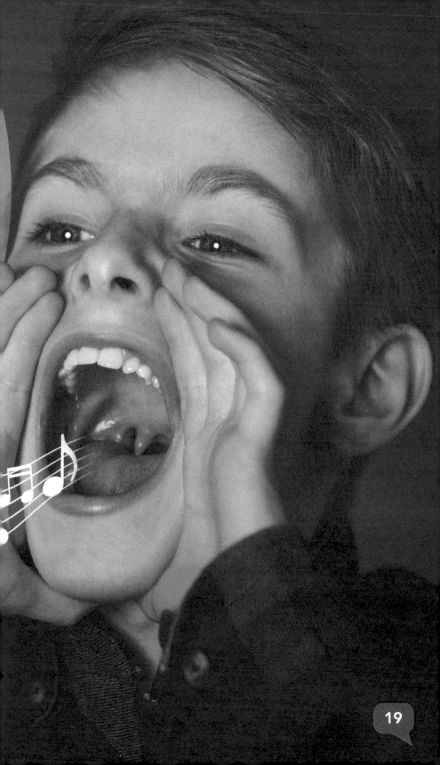

Different parts of the mouth make different sounds. Sounds such as *s*, *sh*, and *t* are made at the front of the tongue. Sounds such as *g*, *h*, and *k* are made at the back of the tongue. Some sounds, such as *b* and *m*, are made with the lips. Some vowel sounds, such as *o*, are made with rounded lips, while others, such as *a*, are not.

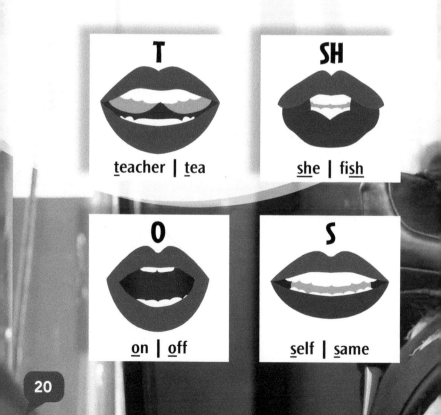

T

teacher | tea

SH

she | fish

O

on | off

S

self | same

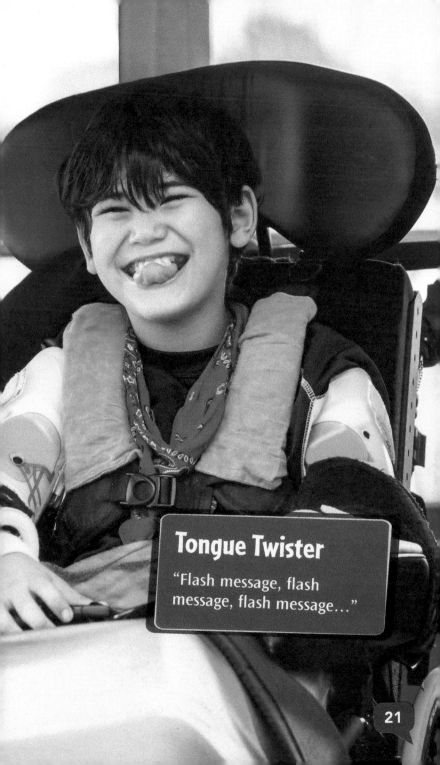

Tongue Twister

"Flash message, flash message, flash message…"

What Goes Wrong

People may think they mess up tongue twisters because their tongues get **clumsy**. But that is not why.

The brain controls speech. Signals for some sounds go to the same part of the tongue. The brain has a hard time signaling two things to the same place at the same time. The tongue stumbles because of the jumbled signals.

Tongue Twister

"Silly Sally swiftly shooed seven silly sheep."

Like to Like

The brain most often flips sounds that are formed in the same part of the mouth. That is why the *s* and *sh* sounds of "She sells seashells" are easily mixed up.

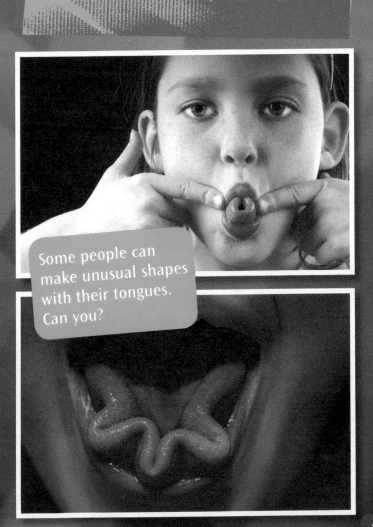

Some people can make unusual shapes with their tongues. Can you?

Stuttering

Stuttering and tongue twisters have one thing in common. They both start in the brain. Scientists are not sure why some people stutter. But they think that speech signals might play a role in it. These signals could come from different parts of the brain in people who stutter than in those who do not. A person who stutters might learn ways to control it.

What Is Stuttering?

Stuttering can mean a person repeats the same sound. Or it can mean a person says the same sound for a long time. It can also mean a person cannot speak a word that he or she normally can say. About five out of every one hundred children have a stutter.

Tongue Twister

"Red rubber baby buggy bumpers bounce."

Twisters Untwisted

What can you do if your tongue gets in a twist? Remember that it all starts in your brain! If you slow down, your brain may be able to send the right signals for clear speech. Practicing helps, too. Your brain can learn something new if you practice. You might even become the next Tongue Twister Take Down champion!

Tongue Twister

"Greek grapes, Greek grapes, Greek grapes…"

A New Champion?

Many people used to think this was the hardest tongue twister:

The sick sixth Sheik's sixth sheep's sick.

But now, scientists think they have found something even harder to say:

Pad kid poured curd pulled cod.

Which do you think is harder to say three times fast?

Glossary

clumsy—moving in an awkward way

instinct—a way of behaving that is natural and not learned

jumbled—in the wrong order or mixed up

organ—important part of the body that has a specific job to do

quipped—said something that was clever

stumbled—spoke or acted in an awkward way

tongue-tied—not able to speak

vibrate—move back and forth quickly in short movements